The Missing

The True Story of
My Family in World War II

For **Emma**, **Elsie**, and **Emile**.
In memory of my father's
"missing" uncles and aunts:
Oscar (Jeschie) and **Rachel**, **Martin**,
Stella and **Bernard**, **Bella**, **Willi**, and **Genia**.

First US paperback edition 2024
First published by Walker Books (UK) 2020

Library of Congress Catalog Card Number 2020918837
ISBN 978-1-5362-1289-1 (hardcover)
ISBN 978-1-5362-3621-7 (paperback)

24 25 26 27 28 29 FRS 10 9 8 7 6 5 4 3 2 1

Printed in Altona, Manitoba, Canada

This book was typeset in Clarendon.

Candlewick Press
99 Dover Street
Somerville, Massachusetts 02144

www.candlewick.com

Michael Rosen

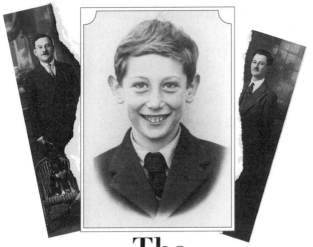

The Missing

The True Story of My Family in World War II

CANDLEWICK PRESS

Not Just for Them

This is about France.

This is about Germany.

This is about Jews.

This is not about France.

This is not about Germany.

This is not about Jews.

This story is about things that happened to my family a long time ago, back when photos and films were in black and white. But when I think about it, my relatives were refugees—a lot like the people you may have seen on the news recently.

Because of the events of the Second World War, they were forced to run: to flee and hide. When I turn on the TV now, eighty years later, I see thousands of families that have been forced to run from new wars, driven into hiding and sometimes losing their lives.

So I hope this book becomes part of a bigger conversation about the refugee crisis. About how to find fair and decent ways of helping people like my relatives.

Michael Rosen

FOREWORD

I was standing in a synagogue in Prague with my sons and my wife, scanning the walls, when I realized what I was seeing. The Pinkas Synagogue lists the names of the Jews of the area who were killed by the Nazis in the Holocaust. Line after line of Czech and German names, dizzying lines of names. And then a few caught my eye, names I'd seen on our family tree, relatives my mother mentioned in a quiet voice, in passing—lost. All I know of them are the names on the wall, the names in our family history. So many of us have stories like that—ancestors we know of, but maybe only a name, or a place of origin, or a fragment of a family story. Whether it is someone who was brought to America from Africa, or fled from a war and changed a name, or entered without papers and did not want to be traced, or was murdered in a concentration camp, we have names without history, or family history without names.

Michael Rosen faced the same dilemma, but he found two pathways to connect with those missing relations. Through careful and painstaking detective work, he did manage to learn about the French and Polish relations he lost to Hitler's death camps. That is one kind of connection, and today, with DNA research and the many sites and organizations that have tools to help with genealogical research—as well as persistence and luck—we can sometimes add whole branches to our family histories. But more than a historian, Michael is a poet. And so in his poetry, his command of words, he could invoke the dead, bring them, and his search for them, to life. He shows us that we need not be defeated by the loss of documents, trails that turn cold. We have the power, now, to imagine, to create, a connection to that missing past.

Within the Pinkas Synagogue in Prague is a permanent exhibition of the art created by children in the Terezín concentration camp—most of those children were later sent to Auschwitz to die. But we can share their dreams and fears and hopes because Friedl Dicker-Brandeis was an artist who believed in encouraging young people's "creative work" and was in Terezín. She gave young people the tools, and the time, to speak through their images. Those images reach out to us, and we can reach back with our creations—as Michael did when he felt his relatives speaking through letters and photographs and he replied with poems.

I see Michael's book as a set of beginnings offered to all of us. He models in his journey the challenges of seeking information where there are blanks. We build a bridge through research and detective work. And he models in his poetry a bridge to the past we can all build through art, not only with words, but with images, music, and dance. We build a bridge in imagination and empathy. We can make the past live for us, both by delving into it and by expressing it through art. That is the gift this book offers.

Marc Aronson

Rutgers University

My Family Tree

Jonas = Marta

France   Poland

Oscar = Rachel   Martin   Willi   Genia   Bella   Bernard = Stella
(Jeschie)

Michael
(Micha)

(Left)
**Rachel
and Oscar**

(Right)
**Michael, Stella,
and Bella**

(Left)
Martin

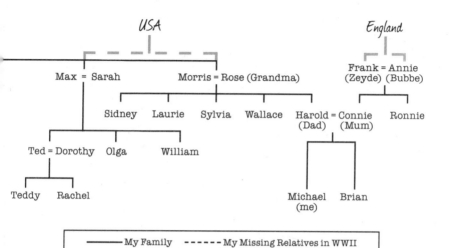

USA   England

Max = Sarah   Morris = Rose (Grandma)   Frank = Annie (Zeyde) (Bubbe)

Sidney   Laurie   Sylvia   Wallace   Harold = Connie (Dad) (Mum)   Ronnie

Ted = Dorothy   Olga   William

Teddy   Rachel

Michael (me)   Brian

———— My Family   - - - - - - My Missing Relatives in WWII

Rose and Morris

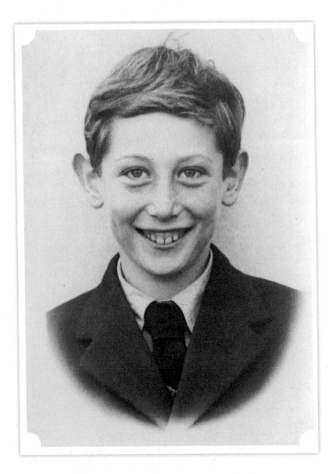

Me aged ten, in Pinner

1

I grew up in a peaceful sort of a place called Pinner, to the north of London—full of people who caught the train to the city in the morning and came back only in the evening.

My family lived in a flat over a shop: me; my mother, Connie; my father, Harold; and my brother, Brian. In the evenings, I played in a stony alleyway at the back of the shop, and every day I walked across the Memorial Park to school with my friend "Harrybo." (His real name was Brian Harrison, but we all called him that.) He and I used to talk about wild animals, insects, the books we had read—and radios. He was mad keen on old radios: he liked to take them apart and put them back together.

Sometimes grown-ups talked about "the War," and they always meant the Second World War. At the time, it seemed to me that the War existed only in the stories they told. I knew a bomb had landed in a park near where we lived. One bomb. That was it.

But quite a few of our dads had been in the army. My dad was American, so he had been in the United States Army. He still had some of his uniform and gear: a cooking pan, a special kind of spade called an entrenching tool, and little brass badges saying **US ARMY**. I loved listening to his stories about his time as a soldier, and I loved the way he put on an exaggerated American accent when he told them.

Dad wasn't ever in a battle. He was sent out to Berlin and told to write reports on the army's time there, so he went round the different bases to find out what was going on. One colonel thought that my dad had come to spy on him—to see if he was doing anything he shouldn't have been.

"Do you like mushrooms?" asked the colonel.

"I do and I don't," said Dad.

"I can give you as many as you want," came the reply, and he took my dad down into the old bomb shelters under the streets . . . where he had built a mushroom farm. He was using the mushrooms as a bribe so that Dad wouldn't put anything about it in his report.

"Thousands of mushrooms!" Dad would say. "Right there, in the middle of a bombed-out city. People were starving, living in cellars, under the rubble—and he was growing mushrooms!"

I would imagine that.

Another time, a friend of my dad's wanted to know what had happened to a colleague who had worked at the Berlin Natural History Museum. It was midwinter, with deep snow everywhere, but my dad still set out to find the museum. As he drew nearer to where it should have been, he could see ruined bits of building sticking up out of the snow—and in between the broken towers, there was the skeleton of a giant dinosaur.

I would imagine that, too.

There was nothing like that round our way. Though one day, a boy came to school and said that he had found an old bomb shelter in the Memorial Park. So when it was getting dark, my friends and I went and levered off the metal cover, then climbed down the ladder into the shelter.

There were beds still with blankets on them and bits of rubbish on the floor. We got scared standing there in the dark and climbed out—but I think maybe we didn't put the metal cover back properly, because, not long afterward, the park wardens put earth over the top of it.

I started to wonder who had been down there and what it had really been like in Pinner during the War.

There were dinosaur skeletons

standing there in the middle of nowhere.

Great bones and skulls

rising up out of the snow

amongst heaps of broken brick

and broken glass.

"I'll never forget the sight

of those dinosaur skeletons,"

my dad said.

I've never forgotten them, either—

though I never saw them.

From **Skeletons**

2

At the weekends, we'd sometimes go and see our relatives. To visit Mum's family, we used to ride on the Metropolitan line in train carriages that had little doors with brass handles.

On the handles, it said *Live in Metro-Land* in beautiful curly writing. Metro-Land was just another name for the area around the Metropolitan line, but I thought it was its own country—separate from London, from England, from the War. I felt proud to live there and memorized the names of stations all the way up to Baker Street, where we had to get off.

From Baker Street, we would catch the bus to Hackney, where Mum's parents (my grandparents) and her brother, Ronnie, lived in a ground-floor flat. We called my grandparents Bubbe and Zeyde, which mean "Granny" and "Granddad" in Yiddish.

Uncle Ronnie was studying physics—he used to help my brother, Brian, with his science homework. Zeyde worked in a factory that made boys' school caps. And Bubbe kept chickens in the yard out the back. She took me to the market to buy bagels and all sorts of other food we didn't eat in Pinner, like chopped herring, chopped liver, and a kind of yogurt called *smetana*.

Zeyde used to take me to a big park called Hackney Downs. That was where he liked to hang around with his friends, who all spoke in Yiddish. They told lots of jokes, and every time I was there, they would say to Zeyde, "Is this your grandson, Frank?"—in English, but with a very strong accent.

"Yes," he'd say.

"Nice-looking boy," they'd reply. Always that. And then they would all laugh.

When we came back from the park, we played games. First we would play checkers . . . and

Zeyde always won. Next we would play chess . . . and Zeyde always won. And then we would play fox and chickens, and guess what? Zeyde always won!

After that, I would ask him to show me the ship in the bottle on the mantelpiece—and wonder how the ship got inside the glass. "Aha!" Zeyde would say . . . and then put the bottle back.

All of a sudden, it would be time to leave. Zeyde would give me and my brother a coin each—though Mum would tell him he shouldn't.

And on the way home, I used to think about the ship sailing along the mantelpiece when we weren't there.

Bagel

On Sundays,

we go over to see Bubbe and Zeyde.

Bubbe takes me to the bagel shop to buy bagels.

There are hundreds and hundreds of them.

Then we take them home.

We sit down to eat the bagels,

and Zeyde says,

"Save the hole for me."

So I eat a bit of the bagel.

Then I say,

"Do you want the hole now, Zeyde?"

And he says, "No, there's too much bagel

round the hole.

I just want the hole."

So I eat some more bagel.

And I say,

"Do you want the hole now, Zeyde?"

And he says, "No, there's too much bagel.

I just want the hole."

So I eat some more

until all that's left is a tiny, tiny little

ring of bagel

round the hole.

And I say, "Do you want the hole now, Zeyde?"

And he says, "No, I can still see some

bagel round the hole."

So then I eat the tiny, tiny ring of bagel

round the hole

and there is no bagel left.

And Zeyde looks at me and says,

"So? You couldn't save me the hole?"

3

My other grandma, my dad's mother, lived in East London with my aunt Sylvia and her husband. Her name was Rose, but my dad called her Ma and we called her Grandma. She was ill by the time we knew her, so she just used to sit there in her chair, watching us all.

Grandma had been born in England, but her parents came from Poland. And while she was living in London, she had met and married a Polish man called Morris—my grandfather. They had two children before moving to Massachusetts, in the USA, where they had three more children.

Then Grandma and Morris split up, and Grandma came back to London with their three youngest children: my dad, Harold; Aunt Sylvia; and their brother Wallace, who sadly died not long after they arrived. Morris and the two eldest children, Sidney and Laurie, stayed in America.

Sometimes, when we sat round the kitchen table, Brian and I would ask Dad about his family. He told us that, after he came to England, he didn't ever see his dad, Morris, again—which seemed to make him very sad.

He told us Morris had a brother Max (Dad's uncle, so my great-uncle). Like Morris, Max migrated from Poland and ended up in America. He got married and had three children: Ted, Olga, and William. Dad hadn't ever met them.

But Morris and Max had six other brothers and sisters. Three sisters and a brother had stayed in Poland, where their parents, Jonas and Marta, were from originally. They were Stella, Bella, Genia, and Willi. Then there were two more brothers who had migrated to France, called Oscar and Martin.

"One of them was a clock mender," Dad said, "and the other one was a dentist."

"What happened to them all—the brothers and sisters in Poland and France?" I asked.

Dad shrugged. "I don't know," he said. "They were there at the beginning of the War, but they had gone by the end. I suppose they died in the camps."

In the camps? I thought. *What camps?*

It made me think of school holidays: we used to go camping, and it nearly always rained . . .

But Dad didn't mean camps like that.

Sometimes, on TV, they used to show what concentration camps were like. They said that hundreds of thousands, probably millions, of people were killed in these camps.

I would lie in bed and think about this. It seemed horrifying. Awful. But I didn't really get it.

Why did they put my great-aunts and great-uncles in these camps? And why did they kill them?

And now they were gone. They had just disappeared—we didn't even have any pictures of them.

All that was left was my dad's shrug.

The Absentees

There are gaps,

there are blanks,

in the house

of my life;

there's a face,

nothing more,

something gone

from my life.

She was here,

he was there,

in the rooms

of my life;

there's a place

for them both

in the words

of my life.

Written for Holocaust Memorial Day, 2018

4

The language my bubbe and zeyde spoke—Yiddish—was Jewish. The food they ate—bagels, chopped herring, chopped liver, *smetana*—was Jewish. Their friends were all Jewish, too.

As far as I know, they weren't religious: they didn't go to synagogue to worship. But they still kept up lots of Jewish traditions, which had been passed on to them by their parents and grandparents and great-grandparents.

In the 1920s, when my grandfather Morris and his brothers and sisters were growing up in Poland, the economy crashed all around the world. Germany was hit hard: people were miserable, and they wanted someone to blame.

And around the same time, Adolf Hitler wrote the book *Mein Kampf* (*My Struggle*), in which he said all of Germany's problems were because of "the Jews." More than that, Hitler and the party he led, the Nazis, said "the Jews" were an inferior race—lesser than "pure" Germans, who he called Aryans.

Even more than that, the Nazis said that not only were Jewish companies driving Germans out of business, but Jewish culture was replacing German culture and traditions.

This is called scapegoating: blaming a person or group of people for something bad that's happened. And when I hear racists in action today, when I hear people saying racist things while pretending that they are being "realistic." I go back to Hitler's speeches where he explained "realistically" that the problem for Germans was the Jews.

The Nazis' racism worked. Once they were in power, they gradually put into place all sorts of laws that targeted Jewish people. This was part of the Nazis' antisemitism—a racism that is directed at Jews.

There were laws to stop Jewish people from

going to university. Laws to stop Jewish people from appearing in public life: as politicians, as entertainers, as doctors.

Eventually there were laws that prevented Jewish people from having jobs and owning property. And then later, during the War, there were laws to take Jewish people from their homes and force them to live in open-air prisons, which some people called ghettos.

This was all leading toward what the Nazis called the Final Solution to the Jewish Question, which they hoped would be the genocide of all the Jews in Europe. *Genocide* is the killing (or attempted killing) of a whole group of people. Today, this genocide is often called the Holocaust.

At the same time, the Nazis targeted other groups of people with a view to killing them all, including Polish people, Roma people, and everyone who they thought had something "wrong" with them genetically.

The Nazis and those who helped them (known as collaborators) rounded people up, sometimes killing them straight away, sometimes enslaving them, often working them to death on farms, in mines and in factories making guns and bombs. They also sent them to ghettos, labor camps, and, toward the end of the War, death camps, where people died from disease or lack of food, or were gassed by "killing machines."

It's incredibly difficult to find out the names of everyone who died, because so many documents were destroyed in the last days of the War. For the same reason, it's also hard to know exactly how many people died. But we know that the Second World War was the deadliest time in human history.

And about fifteen million people were killed during the Holocaust. Nearly six million of these people were Jews.

When they do war,
they forget how to count.
They forget how to count,
and that's how they do it.

They come,
they kill;
they kill,
they go.

No numbers.
No names.
They disappear them.
They vanish them.
That's how they do it.

They come,
they kill;
they kill,
they go.

And it's
"worth it,"
they say,
"it's worth it, believe us,"
if you forget how to count.

If you forget the numbers.
If you forget the names.
If you forget the faces.

When they do war,
they forget how to count.
They forget how to count,
and that's how they do it.

But we're counting.
Watch us:
we're counting.
Listen.
We're counting.
And
we count.

From **Counting**

5

My mum and dad were teachers, which meant that we had long summer holidays. We camped in Wales and Yorkshire, and sometimes we went abroad. I remember holidays all over France: in Brittany in the north, the Jura Mountains in the east, the Pyrénées in the south, and the Ardèche in the middle.

I loved France so much that for a while I wanted to be French! I loved the mountains and I loved the beaches. I loved the smell of herbs like thyme on the hillsides. I started to learn how to speak French, and I loved the language. I started to like French food and learn French songs. I bought French clothes and tried to look French.

When I was a teenager, I stayed for six weeks in a kids' summer camp called a *colonie de vacances*. I was the only English person there and spoke only French for the entire time. We played football, table tennis, and volleyball, climbed mountains, and went canoeing. I learned all sorts of slang words, like *la flotte* for water, and *les godasses* for shoes. When we went canoeing, we paddled through a gorge where no one lived and saw eagles flying round the rocks.

I liked studying the big insects and mini-beasts in France: the praying mantis, the flying grasshoppers, the scorpions . . . When I got lonely, I wrote to Mum and Dad and told them how I was getting on. I told them there was no road to the *colonie*: we had to cross the river on a little chariot hanging from wires. We used to dive off it into the river.

And I told them how we once went for a midnight hike and came to a special monument high up in the mountains. It marked where the Nazis had killed the men from the village during the War, and everyone went quiet when we looked at it.

I was sad to come home, so the next year, I went to France again. I traveled all over and met up with a French family who had a holiday place high up in the Pyrenees. For several summers, I stayed there and helped them with the harvest—I even learned some words in the language they spoke there, which they called *patois* and wasn't the same as the French I'd learned in school.

Over the years, I kept going back to France, learning more French and reading lots of French books. Which is a big part of why I started to wonder about my two great-uncles Oscar and Martin—the ones who, out of all those brothers and sisters, had ended up in France.

I wanted to know more—and not just because I could speak French, which meant I could look through French records without a translator. It was also because their stories were tied up with this country that I loved. A country that had suffered during the War.

France joined the Allies in 1939, soon after

the Nazis invaded Poland; less than a year later, the Nazis invaded France and, in six short weeks, seized control of Paris.

At first, they tried to behave "legally"—as they saw it, of course. They made a deal with the French government and divided the country in two: there was one part that the Nazis occupied, stationing their troops there and ruling over it, and another that was run by a new French government.

This was called the Vichy government, because it was based in the city of Vichy. It was meant to be independent—though it was really overseen by the German army. And it turned out that some of the French people in power shared Nazi ideas about the Jews: they wanted to "Francify" France, like the Nazis wanted to make Germany more German.

And they wanted to do it by removing any Jewish influences.

It is illegal in France to list people who are French citizens by their religion. So the Vichy officials made lists of Jews who were living in France but had been born somewhere else.

And they handed those lists over to the Nazis.

OCCUPIED FRANCE 1940–1942

I'm not on the list

I'm not on the list.
I'm not on the list.
All I have to do
is tell them if I know someone
who should be on the list.

If I don't
tell them that I know someone
who should be on the list,
then I'll be on a list of people
who don't help them make the list.

And people in my family
will be on a list of people
in families of people
who don't help them make the list
of people who should be on the list.

If you're not on the list,
or the list of the people
who don't help them make the list,
or the list of people who know people who
don't help them make the list . . .
you're OK.
It's all OK.
It's going to be all right.

6

I really wanted to find out more about Oscar and Martin, but there wasn't much to go on. So I decided to take a trip to America and visit my relatives over there.

By that time, my grandfather Morris had died and so had his brother Max. But Max's son and daughter Ted and Olga were alive and well.

I stayed with Ted and his wife in Manchester, Connecticut. Ted told me stories about Morris: how he used to come and stay with his family, how he drove a convertible, and how he had five smart suits that he kept in a trunk.

I met Olga at a big party that Ted's children, Teddy and Rachel, had organized for him. (It was his birthday, but the party was meant to be a surprise, so we all had to pretend we'd come to celebrate Hanukkah!)

When I asked her about her French uncles, Oscar and Martin, Olga told me she used to write to them when she was a girl.

Wow! Suddenly here was a tiny bit of information about them.

"Did they answer?" I said. "Have you got any of the letters they sent you?"

She said no. "I wrote to them to teach myself French."

Trying not to feel too disappointed, I asked, "Where did they live?"

"I think it was a place called Metz," she said. "And maybe, another time—a place nearby—Nancy. One of them was a clock mender, and the other was a dentist. I'm not sure which was which."

That was just what my dad had told me. "Anything else?"

She thought for a moment. "I think they lived in a street called rue de Thionville."

Now I had something: a clue.

When I got home, I looked up "rue de Thionville" and I found that there were quite a few of them— there's a town called Thionville in northeastern France, and any number of roads in or out of its center are called by the same name.

I went online and searched for "Oscar Rosen," "Martin Rosen," "rue de Thionville," "Metz," "Nancy". . . I tried all sorts of different ways of phrasing it, over months and months.

But no matter what I tried, nothing came up.

In the family, they were always the French uncles.

The ones who were there before the war.

The ones who weren't there after the war.

The family said that one of them was a dentist

and the other one mended clocks. **And that was it.**

Not quite it. There was a street that the relatives

here and in America talked about, which was

"rue de Thionville." And places in France:

"Nancy" and "Metz." And one of the brothers

was Oscar and the other was Martin. **And that was it.**

Though Olga, in America, nearly as small as a walnut,

said that she used to write letters to them to learn

how to write French.

And that was it.

But I wouldn't let it go.

From **Not Just for Them**

At the Wiener Library in 2018

7

I went down all sorts of different paths, every one of which turned out to be a dead end.

For instance, around that time, I was in an airport waiting for a plane and got talking to a young French guy. He said he was from Metz, so I told him I was trying to find out things about my lost relatives, and I thought one or the other—or both—lived there before the War.

He was a student and knew how to find out about things like that, so we swapped emails.

A few weeks later, I got a message—I rushed to open it. This could be it, the big breakthrough. I scrolled through his email and . . . nothing. He hadn't found a thing!

Eventually, I had to admit that I'd reached a full stop. There was just nothing—no information about Oscar and Martin. So, to distract myself, I started to read more about what happened in Europe toward the end of the War.

I read how, to the Nazis' twisted minds, there were two purposes to the Holocaust: to remove people, but also to remove the memory of them. They were convinced that Jewish people had destroyed European culture, so they wanted to remove all Jewish influences from art and music and literature.

They looted and destroyed work by Jewish artists and art collections belonging to Jewish families. They burned thousands and thousands of books they had decided were "un-German."

Before starting my research, I knew the War had spanned several continents and lasted six years (1939–1945). During that time, many different countries were involved, including all the countries in what was called the British Empire.

On June 6, 1944, Britain and America, along with troops from Canada, invaded France on what became known as D-Day. They pushed back the German army, and the French Resistance freed Paris and other parts of France.

Germany ended up fighting on two fronts: the Russians were advancing from the east and the Americans, British, and Canadians from the west.

When the Nazis knew they were losing, they wanted to hide what they had done. They destroyed some of the camps they had built—and they tried to destroy any evidence that the millions and millions of people they had killed ever existed.

As I read this, I felt so angry and sad that I hadn't found a way to remember Oscar and Martin. No one in my family knew anything about them, and this frustrated me beyond words. It meant the Nazis had succeeded. And the last thing I wanted was for them to have won.

So now I really, really wanted to know more. *They can't get away with this,* I said to myself.

Names

When we talk about sisters and brothers
and fathers and mothers
and we get to the sisters and brothers of my father's father,
my dad shuts his eyes and says he'd rather not talk about that.

But we ask for their names
and where they are,
where do they live and is it far?
And bit by bit he tells us their names
and that none of them are alive—
there was a war, he explains.

And we sit and we think about us sitting here,
how sisters and brothers could just disappear,
but because Mum and Dad were in a different place,
they could stay here where they were safe.
My mother and father were able to survive,
and here we are now and we're all alive.

8

One day, entirely out of the blue, an email arrived from America.

It was from Teddy—the son of Max's son Ted, who I had stayed with in Connecticut. And Teddy had news. Not any old news: big news.

When Teddy was a little boy, Ted had split up with Teddy's mother, Dorothy. Her brother— Teddy's uncle—had just died, and among his papers were four letters. Do you know who they were from?

Amazingly and incredibly, two of them were from Oscar! Teddy scanned the letters and sent them to me, and I pored over them.

The first thing I noticed was Oscar's address: *11 rue Mellaise, Niort.* Niort? That's on the other side of France from Metz, where everyone said that he and Martin lived! It's more than four hundred miles away, far over to the west.

The letters are all written to Max—Oscar's brother.

CARTE POSTALE

Exp.
Rosen,11 rue Meilaise
NIORT (Deux Sévres)
    France

Sonst kein Neues,als ich
Euch herzlich grüsse und
küsse,Euer denkender Oscar.
Von meiner 1.Frau folgen an
Euch viele Grüsse

Monsieur

Max R o s e n

96,West Cedar St.

B o s t o n

U. S. A.   Mass

                              Niort le 18-3-1940.
    Meine Lieben.
    Euren L.Brief v.17-1-1940, habe ich erhalten,es freut
mich dass Ihr gesund seid und das Gleiche kann ich Euch
mitteilen. Auch hoffe ich dass Ihr mein Schreiben V.6/2
erhalten habet. Nur wundert mich sehr dass Ihr an mich
so wenig schreibt. So wie kann ich Euch mitteilen, dass
ich aus Polen noch immer kein Lebenszichen erhalten ha-
be. Jetzt frage ich Euch an ob Ihr schon ein Schreiben
aus Polen bekommen habet,falls ja, so bitte mir eine
Copie (nicht das Original) einzusenden. Ich bitte Euch
nochmals und gibt mir sofort Bescheid.
    Was anbelangt mein Geschäft,kann ich Euch mitteilen,
dass ich schon seit den 20/8-1939, nicht schaffe und das
wir von den Ersparnissen leben. Es wird täglich in der C
Cassa weniger.
    Deinen L.Brief habe ich an Martin eingeschickt.
    Es freut mich dass Du 1.Bruder nach Polen Geld schicks
leider kann ich dasselbe nicht tun.

Rosen
96 West Cedar St.
Boston Mas

From:

Rosen, 11 rue Mellaise
Niort (Deux Sévres)
France

To:

Monsieur Max Rosen
96 West Cedar St.
Boston, Mass U.S.A.

March 18, 1940

My dears,

I have received your dear letter
dated January 17, 1940. I am glad
that you are healthy and I can tell
you the same about us. I also hope
that you received my letter dated
February 6, 1940. But I am very
surprised that you write to me so
little. I can inform that I have
still not received a sign of life
from Poland. Now I am asking you
whether you have already received a

letter from Poland. If yes, please send me a copy (not the original). I am asking you again and let me know immediately.

As for my business, I can tell you that since August 20, 1939, I have not worked and that we live from our savings. Our money is getting less every day.

I forwarded your dear letter to Martin.

I am glad that you are sending money to our dear brother.

I am pleased to hear that you, dear brother, send money to Poland.

Unfortunately I cannot do the same.

Otherwise no news. I am sending you heartfelt greetings and kisses.

Your Oscar who is thinking of you. My dear wife sends many regards.

My dears,

Only today did I receive your dear letter dated February 29. I hope that you already received my card dated March 18. We are glad to hear that you are in good health and I can tell you the same from us. We were very pleased to receive your letter and we thank you very much.

I just learned from you that dear Bella is no more in Biała. I tried to make enquiries, but unfortunately I can't get any information.

I am very surprised that you have not yet received any news from Poland. You live in a neutral country, therefore it is much easier for you to find out something about our sisters in Poland. Who knows whether they are still alive.

Write immediately. Also let me know right away whether you received this card. You may also write to me in Yiddish. I learned that it is best to write in Polish to Poland,

and up to 25 words, not more. If you
receive a letter from Poland, *only*
send me a *copy*.

Nothing else new, as I am awaiting
good news.

Best regards, your brother,
brother-in-law,

Oscar

My dear wife also sends you many
regards and wishes you the best.
Awaiting immediate answers, as it
takes very long.

Oscar couldn't earn any money because, along
with millions of other French people, he'd fled
from eastern France to western France. He
and his wife had been surviving on whatever
savings they had—for seven months.

They must have been very scared for the
future. But more than anything else, Oscar
sounds desperate to find out what's happened to

his brother and three sisters in Poland—he must have had a sense that the situation was even worse over there.

That's not all—Teddy had found another two letters from Oscar's sister Stella and her husband, Bernard. They had been living in west Poland with their son, Michael, at the beginning of the War.

Michael was just seventeen when Poland was invaded—by the Nazis to the west and the Soviets to the east.

Stella and Bernard were desperate to do something for Michael—and both letters to Max beg him to "take my only child."

From:

Rechnitz

Dombrowa 6/S

Schlesische Str. 14

To:

Mr. Max Rosen

96 West Cedar

Boston, Mass U.S.A.

January 22, 1941

Dear Brother,

I have written to you several times and urged you fervently to take in my only child, Micha Rechnitz in Joszkar—6 Ta, Maryjskoja U.S.S.R. pocstowy Jasscryk No. 8 barack / 7. Soviet Union.

He was sent away from Lemberg and only America can rescue him. Therefore I am fervently asking you to take the necessary steps immediately. Many thousands have already gone to America. I am asking you again to fulfill my request. I have sent you my son's birth certificate. Born November 16, 1923, in Dombrowa 6/S.

What are you doing, my dears? Kisses to you and your dear wife.

Maybe for now you can send him a few dollars? I beg you very much.

February 11, 1941

Dear Brother,

I hope you have already taken the steps to take in my son. Maybe you could adopt him to make this work?

Dear brother, I urge you. For now send him a few dollars and packages with food because he has nothing. I fervently urge you to send something as soon as possible. Don't be upset with me but only you . . . [remainder of the sentence obscured by airmail stamp]

Kisses to you and to your dear wife and children.

Your sister,
Stella

Thousands of Jewish people tried to make their way to America, just as Stella says. But while some succeeded, many more were turned away—as they were by governments all over Europe.

One of the most famous examples is from 1939, when a ship called the *St. Louis* set sail from Nazi Germany carrying more than nine hundred Jewish refugees. The ship made it all the way to Cuba, a trip of some four thousand miles . . . only for the US government to send it and its passengers all the way back to Europe.

Stella is frantic to do something for her only son: a seventeen-year-old Jewish boy whose world is falling apart all around him and who will surely die if he stays with his family in west Poland.

But did the letters work? What happened to Micha (Michael)?

This part of the puzzle I knew already.

Not long after the end of the War, there was a knock on my aunt Sylvia's door in London. A young man was standing on her doorstep.

"Lady Sylvia?" he asked.

She let him in—and, bit by bit, it became clear that the young man was Michael!

We don't know whether Max tried and failed to get him to America, but in the end, Stella and Bernard put Michael on an eastbound train to get him away from the Nazis.

When Michael arrived in the Soviet half of Poland, he was sent to a prison camp in Russia. But then, in 1941, the Nazis decided they wanted to control *all* of Poland, not just the west—so they fought their way east, and their alliance with the Soviets crumbled to bits.

Michael was offered the chance to join a new Polish Free Army, fighting on the side of the Soviets—who had gone over to the Allies' side. And he accepted. He traveled thousands of miles with them, fighting battle after battle, all the way to Italy.

When the War was over, Michael didn't want to go back to Poland. Everyone knew by then that all the Jews had gone from Poland. Nearly all of them killed. So he thought he would try to get to America to find his relatives there: his uncles Morris and Max.

In the end, he got only as far as London, where he stayed with Sylvia. He went on to become

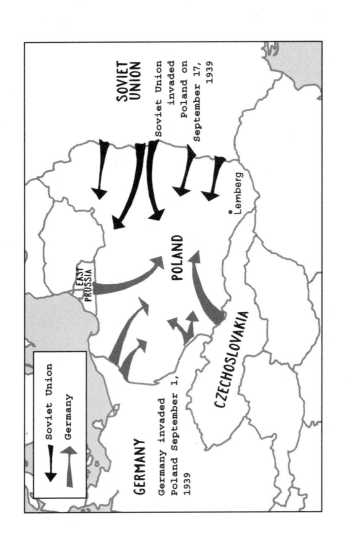

SOVIET UNION

Soviet Union invaded Poland on September 17, 1939

EAST PRUSSIA

POLAND

Lemberg

CZECHOSLOVAKIA

GERMANY

Germany invaded Poland September 1, 1939

Soviet Union

Germany

a taxi driver, got married, and had children of his own.

Michael never saw his parents, Stella and Bernard, again. He never found out what happened to them. All he had was one photo of his mother . . . and now, these letters.

But it was because of their actions that he survived.

On the Move Again

You know
you gotta go.
No time to grieve.
You just gotta leave.
Get away from the pain.
On the move again.

Take the train.
Catch a plane.

Make the trip
in a ship.

Take a hike.
Ride a bike.

Go by car.
Going far.

Use your feet
on the street.

Get stuck
in a truck.

Then you arrive
and you're alive.

You arrive.
You're alive.

What you leave behind
won't leave your mind.

But home is where you find it.
Home is where you find it.
Home is where you find it.
Home is where you find it.

9

I went back to the two letters from Oscar and looked at the address he had sent them from . . . and then, straightaway, I searched for "11 rue Mellaise, Niort" online.

Incredibly, the house was still standing. But why had Oscar and his wife been living there, not in Metz?

I looked up what had been happening in France in 1940, the year Oscar wrote to Max. I found out that when France was invaded by the German army, which came marching in from the east, millions of people fled to the west and the south of the country—from places like Metz in the northeast to places like Niort in the west.

In France it's called L'Exode, or the Exodus, which is the name in the Bible given to the time when the Jews fled from Egypt.

Now I knew that Oscar had left eastern France to get away from the Nazis. But I wanted to know what happened to the Jewish people in Niort. Was there any way of finding out?

I searched and found a book called *Les Chemins de la honte: Itinéraire d'une persécution*, by a man called Jean-Marie Pouplain. The title means "Paths of shame: The road to a persecution."

I ordered it and waited ages for it to arrive—so long that I was sure it had gotten lost in the post. But it did appear eventually, just as my family and I were packing up all our things.

We were leaving a house I had lived in for twenty-five years. Surrounded by big boxes, I ripped open the package and turned straight to the index. There I saw that the name Rosen was mentioned on fourteen different pages.

The first time was on page 34. I quickly flipped to there—even as the moving truck pulled into our drive—and in a list of names that I could see were Jewish, it said in French:

Rosen, Jeschie, né le 23 juin, 1895, polonais,
bonneterie, marié à Kesler, Rachel, née en
1910, 11 rue Mellaise.

This means:

Rosen, Jeschie, born June 23, 1895, Polish,
sock and stocking seller, married to Kesler,
Rachel, born in 1910, 11 rue Mellaise.

It was the right address, and the age fitted. So even though it was "Jeschie" Rosen and not Oscar Rosen, surely this was my father's uncle?

I looked up "Jeschie" and found that it's often a nickname taken from the Hebrew name Yehoshua. Jews who belong to a synagogue are given a special Jewish name as well as their legal one, so I wondered if maybe Oscar's Jewish name had been Yehoshua and people liked to call him Jeschie.

It was just a guess, but it felt right.

I went through the rest of the book while my family waited impatiently for me to get into the car. It really was time for us to move to our new house! But I just couldn't tear myself away.

On one of the pages, it said that Jeschie Rosen was an *horloger de carillon*—a "mender of chiming clocks." That fitted the family story that one of the brothers was a clock mender. . . . But it seemed that Jeschie had been forced to make a living selling socks and stockings, even though he was trained in mending clocks.

I read that the local official—the "prefect" or "subprefect"—had drawn up lists of Jewish people. They were forced to wear a yellow star labeled JUIF ("Jew") and had to put up a sign saying ENTREPRISE JUIVE ("Jewish business") where they worked.

I was horrified. I knew about the yellow stars, and I'd thought about what it must have been like to be marked out by the government as some kind of inferior being. But I didn't know about the "Jewish business" label, and I couldn't believe how dangerous that was. They would have been a target for anyone who wanted to attack them for being Jewish.

On another page in the book, I found the word *forain* next to Jeschie's name, which usually means someone selling things in a market: I pictured him with that sign on his market stall and that badge on his jacket.

Perhaps even worse, the book said that at the time, everything Jews owned—every bit of it— was "Aryanized."

That word . . . *Aryanized*. It means something horrible. It means that everything Jeschie and his wife owned stopped being "Jewish" and was made "Aryan." It means that all their belongings were taken away and given to the government in Vichy France.

Now I was disgusted. But what had actually happened to Oscar-Jeschie? I still didn't know.

I noticed that the rest of the people on the list with Oscar were shipped from Niort to a place near Paris called Drancy . . . and then to Auschwitz, a place where most of them had been killed.

I had another book called *The Deportation of the Jews from France*, and I had often looked in it trying to find Martin and Oscar. There were several different Martin and Oscar Rosens, but I had no way of knowing if any of them could have been my father's uncles.

But this time I was looking up a much less common name: Jeschie. And, sure enough, there he was—in a list of people who were all part of the same convoy.

This is what the book said:

Convoy 62, a convoy of 1,200 Jews leaving Paris-Bobigny at 11:50 a.m. on November

20, 1943. Arrived Auschwitz, November 25,
as cabled by SS Colonel Liebehenschel. 1181
arrived. There had been 19 escapees, they
were young people, who escaped at 8:30 p.m.
near Lérouville. In the convoy there were 83
children who were less than twelve years old.
Out of the convoy 241 were selected for work
and given numbers 164427–164667. Women
numbered 69036–69080 were selected too.
914 were gassed straightaway. In 1945, there
were 29 survivors, 27 men and 2 women.

Here was the horrific reason why my dad,
all those years earlier, had shrugged and said,
"They were there at the beginning of the War,
but they had gone by the end."

I stared at the word "convoy." It meant a
train of cattle trucks with all those people—
men, women, and children—squeezed inside.
Pulling out of a station in Paris and taking five

days to travel through France, across Germany, and into Poland: a journey of more than nine hundred miles.

I searched for more information about Convoy 62 and eventually found a memoir written by a man called Henry Bily—one of the other prisoners on board. Here is his description of the awful journey:

[T]he children cried endlessly. They were hungry, they were afraid, and they were tired. They had never been through such a nightmare, or experienced such a stench. Or such a noise! How many hours had passed? Already, half of the people in our truck seemed completely listless. Of the other half, how many were even lucid? As for me, after finishing the bread that I was given at the beginning of our journey, I was beginning to feel very hungry. . . .

Each of us tried to guess where we were. Each
of us tried to imagine our final destination.
What would be our fate? It would be useless to
recall everything that took place during that
terrible journey. The spread of misinformation
and lies, the smell of the lavatory bucket in
the middle of the truck, and the unbearable
overcrowding, made us no longer quite
human.

—Translated from *Destin à Part: Seul déporté*
rescapé de la rafle de Clans du 25 octobre 1943
by Henry Bily

As I read these words, I wondered about the
"young people" who had managed to escape. I
wondered how they did that; perhaps forcing the
door open and jumping out?

And I thought about the people who hadn't

managed to escape. Who had arrived at this horrific destination, Auschwitz . . . a huge place, which was in different parts a camp, a factory, a forced-labor prison, and an "extermination" center.

I thought of the films I had seen of people being separated, lined up, and marched off in different directions. The awful huts with people dying of starvation and disease. The gas chambers and crematoria—killing people by gassing them and then burning their bodies.

I was overwhelmed by the idea that it could have happened to my father's uncle, his wife, and probably his brother.

They had spent long, happy years living in eastern France, only to be driven from their home and killed, one way or another, in this awful place.

There was something else: in this book, it said that Jeschie was born in Oświęcim.

Do you know what that means? Oświęcim is the Polish word for "Auschwitz."

The terrible truth is that Jeschie was born in the same town where the Nazis built their camp.

I wondered when it was he realized that the death camp he was going to was so near his home.

People run away from war.

Sometimes we get away.

Sometimes we don't.

Sometimes we're helped.

Sometimes we aren't.

From **People Run**

10

I thought perhaps now I had all the information I would ever have about my missing relatives. But I went on searching online.

One day, up popped the names of Oscar and his wife, Rachel—on a monument and in some papers from a French town called Sedan.

There was even a picture of the monument, showing an engraved list of the names of people who were "victims of Nazi barbarism."

Why were they on a monument in a Jewish cemetery in Sedan? No one in the family had ever mentioned Sedan—it's in northern France, close to Belgium. So who had put their names there?

The author of the papers was a man called Gérald Dardart. I wrote to him, and he told me that Oscar and Rachel had lived in Sedan, but when they were picked up by the Nazis, they were in Nice. That's the town in the south of France, pronounced "neece."

And Gérald Dardart said they were arrested by the Nazis in a hotel.

Once again, I needed books to find out more . . . and what I found out was utterly sad.

Nice and its surrounding area wasn't occupied by the Germans during the Second World War but by one of the other Axis powers: Italy. And it seems that while the Nazis were deporting Jews from the rest of France, the Italians were not. More than that: when the Nazis asked the Italians to hand over Jews living in Nice and nearby, they refused.

And even more than that: in Nice there lived a Jewish-Italian man called Angelo Donati, who was doing everything he could to evacuate Jewish refugees. He was working on a risky plan to save about thirty thousand people. He had been trying to organize passports via his British and American contacts, and he had even gotten hold of four ships to carry people to safety.

So how had Oscar and Rachel been captured and sent to Auschwitz?

Well, at the very moment my great-uncle arrived in Nice, the Allies were about to conquer Italy. Donati heard the news and sent a message to the American general Dwight D. Eisenhower, begging him not to announce the victory until he had gotten all the Jews out of Nice. Donati feared that the Nazis would retaliate by invading Nice and capturing Jewish people.

But I'm afraid to say that Eisenhower *did* announce the Allies' victory, and three days later, in September 1943, the Nazis marched into Nice.

And where were the Jews, including Oscar and Rachel? In hotels all over the city, waiting for Donati to get them out. Lots of them weren't even hiding: they were so sure they were going to be rescued.

The Nazis seized them and sent them north to a camp in a housing estate called Drancy. From there, they were sent to the train station Paris-Bobigny. . . .

And you know the rest.

Just another few days, and Oscar and Rachel would have escaped on the boats that Donati had ready and waiting for them.

I felt incredibly sad. They had been so close to being safe and staying alive.

Later I went to the Wiener Library in London to see if they had a list of Jewish people arrested at the Hotel Excelsior at that time. They pulled out a sheet of paper—and on it were Oscar and Rachel Rosen.

Again, I thought about Oscar and Rachel escaping across France to Nice. A journey of more than six hundred miles. Maybe they had heard rumors: "You'll be safe in Nice!" "You'll be able to escape!" Somehow or another, they got there.

Nearly free. So nearly free. But the net had closed around them.

Dear Oscar

What did you think,
as you and Rachel
sat on the floor
of the cattle truck
as it left Paris?

Did you think of the watches
and clocks you had mended?
Did you think of the tiny springs and wheels?

You with your magnifying glass
in your eye, poring over the works
so that a monsieur or a madame
could tell the time,
correct to the exact second . . .

Did you look
through the gaps in the slats
on the side of the truck?

Did you see farmers in fields?
Women selling clothes in a market?

Did you call out?
Did you push your hands through the gaps?

Did the night come creeping in?
Did you see a light from a window
where people sat and
ate their evening meal?

Did you see, in the dark,
horror on Rachel's face?
Did she see horror on yours?

Did you shut her eyes?

Did she shut yours?

Thinking of children

who shut their eyes to make

the world go away?

And then

behind your eyelids

did you think of the cattle

that had once stood in the truck

as they were taken away

to the slaughterhouse?

11

With all these new details, I had another dig about online . . . and I discovered something really quite troubling.

I found a form dated February 1939—it had been filled out by my father's cousin Olga. And it turned out she had tried to get Oscar out of France before the War and had been asking for him to come to America.

This was both amazing and amazingly sad. Because, of course, he never went.

I asked the people who put this file on the Internet if they knew whether the American authorities said that they would let Oscar in. They had no idea.

So I don't actually know whether they said yes or no. I don't know whether the US government offered him a place in America and he refused, or whether they turned him down. But a lot of Jews had their applications rejected. There were all sorts of papers to fill out and hoops to jump through to be accepted—and it would have taken a near miracle for Jewish refugees to tick all those boxes, even as their own government was stripping them of their rights as citizens.

There was something else. When Olga wrote asking for Oscar to come, she called him . . . Jeschie!

Finally I had proof that people in the family called Oscar both "Oscar" and "Jeschie."

That solved *that* one, then—but I was left wondering why Olga had never told me she had tried to get Oscar-Jeschie to come and live with them in America.

She told me she'd written to him to improve her French, but she never told me that. Why not?

Teddy, her nephew, thought it was because she felt guilty. The same reason why, mysteriously, the letters from France and Poland had been hidden away.

It was because the American brothers—my

grandfather Morris and his brother Max—were ashamed. And so were Max's children, Ted and Olga.

The brothers hadn't kept in touch with the rest of their siblings during the War. At its end, when they wondered what had happened to them all—to Oscar, Martin, Bella, Stella, Genia, and Willi—they had "disappeared."

The only one they knew had escaped was Stella's son, Michael. He was the one who had turned up in London after the War—with no intention of returning to Poland.

So my family clammed up and said as little as they could.

I don't blame them. Of course I don't.

It was so important to me that we found out about Oscar—that we remembered him. But I can see how it was just too much for the others. They must have felt devastated at the realization that they had lost so many members of their family. Traumatized, on their relatives' behalf.

And they must have wished that they could have done more. Or perhaps felt that they *should* have done more.

12

And that was it.

Well . . . not quite!

Once again, I thought I had gotten to the end of my trail: found out all that I could. But a few years later, I got an email from Teddy in America. He said that his father, Ted, had died at age 103, and Teddy had gone into his old house.

It was the place where Ted had told me about my grandfather Morris and his five suits.

Teddy said he found a cupboard that was locked. Inside were thousands of photos—and among these was a box labeled "Family Photos." He opened it up . . .

. . . and inside were pictures of our great-uncle Oscar! And his brother Willi and sister Stella, too, as well as their parents.

These photos had been in there the whole time when I came to the house and talked to Ted about the family.

Another picture was of my great-aunt Stella with her son, Michael. They were walking together down a street in Poland.

I quickly got in touch with Michael's son and sent it to him. He said his father was "mesmerized" by the photo. He stared and stared at it.

I hope it wasn't too much of a shock for him, to look at that photo. It was the first time he had ever seen it, and it's only the second photo he has of his mother. He took the first photo with him when he said goodbye to his parents at the beginning of the War.

Several photos of Oscar show him in uniform. At first I thought it must be a French uniform, but I posted the picture on Twitter, along with the information on the back of it.

Do you know what someone told me?

Oscar is wearing a uniform of the Austro-Hungarian Army—one that belonged to a regiment put together in Poland during the First World War. What's more, when I looked up the regiment, I found out that they fought in more than thirty-five battles alongside the German army.

Before he went to France, Jeschie Rosen had been a war hero—on the side of the Germans. A Polish man who had helped the Germans to fight a war.

I shake my head every time I think about that.

Because when it came to the Nazis deciding to get rid of the Jews, this counted for nothing.

I found these things out in order to know.

I found these

things out, I know now, in order to tell other

people.

I found these things out so that Jeschie and

Rachel will be known.

But in the end I know that the point of them

being known is

that this is a story not just for them and

about them.

From **Not Just for Them**

13

What about the second uncle, Martin? The other one living in France?

I couldn't help but carry on looking. I had wrapped up my discoveries about Oscar—and was just putting the finishing touches on this book!—when suddenly I discovered a website with a clue about what happened to Martin.

From 1943 onward, he was living in an area of western France called the Vendée. And in 1944, the Germans sent an instruction to the French officials in the Vendée.

The police were ordered to go out in the middle of the night and arrest the Jews in the area. That meant everyone with a Jewish connection: if someone had one Jewish and one non-Jewish parent, that person would be arrested, too.

The people arrested were told to bring winter clothes, money, and valuables. And the places where they had been staying should be sealed.

I wrote to a specialist library in the Vendée

and asked them to send me any report that mentioned Martin Rozen or Rosen. Almost immediately, they sent me back a report dated January 31, 1944—which told me the following.

At 2:30 in the morning, four police officers arrived at a property owned by someone called Madame Bobières, in the village of Sainte-Hermine.

This property was the living quarters of "Martin Rozen."

The officers' report was full of details. They said that Martin was a jeweler—not a dentist, as I had always been told.

They said that he was five feet, four inches tall, with brown eyes, an oval face, a straight nose, and a regular mouth.

He was dressed in yellow cotton trousers and a gray cotton jacket, wearing a Basque beret and low-heeled shoes.

He had a scar on his left cheek.

I tried to picture the scene: a little village in the countryside; four policemen in their dark blue uniforms turning up in the middle of the night, knocking on the door of a lady's house, and then taking my great-uncle away.

Why?

The report said that Martin had been the one to answer the door that night. What did he think was going on? What did he think was going to happen to him? Was he hiding in Madame Bobières's house? Did he think he was safe in this little village, far away from the cities and the soldiers?

Had he heard about Jews being taken away and never coming back?

Reading it made me feel desperate. How powerless Martin must have felt . . . Had he been angry? Or scared? Or both?

And I thought of the policemen. Didn't they think it was terrible, to arrest someone just because he was Jewish? Somehow, they had gone back to the police station and written such detailed notes, all about what Martin looked like and what he was wearing.

What did they do then? Have breakfast? What did they say to their families? "We arrested a Jew tonight."

Or were they sorry? Sad? Guilty?

According to the report, Martin was taken to the parish hall in a town called La Roche-sur-Yon. Along with thirty other Jews arrested that night, he was put on a train to the nearby town of La Rochelle, then to a nearby city called Poitiers, then to the Drancy internment camp.

The same camp where his brother Oscar and sister-in-law Rachel had been kept, just two and a half months earlier. Though I don't think Martin could possibly have known that . . .

On February 10, 1944, Martin was put on a train of cattle trucks called Convoy 68. There were fifteen hundred people on that train.

No one knew where the train was going—the guards wouldn't tell them. So people called their destination Pitchipoï: a nonsense name.

But it was really headed for Auschwitz.

I found a book written by a woman called Ida Grinspan, who was on the same convoy. She was fourteen years old at the time, and she describes what it was like on those trucks.

How there were families, with children. How the truck was so full, there was no room to sit down. How there was nowhere to go to the toilet. How there was a terrible smell.

When the train arrived at Auschwitz, 210 men and sixty-one women were selected to be killed immediately. Of the fifteen hundred people, forty-two survived.

Martin was never seen again.

That wasn't all. Another paper the Vendée library had sent told me that, a month and a half after Martin's arrest, his landlady Madame

Bobières wrote to the officials telling them how the police had come to her house and arrested a lodger who had been staying with her for more than a year: "Mr. Rosen of Jewish nationality."

"Jewish nationality"? There was no such thing! But this was the first I'd heard that Martin had been staying in this village for a year. Which made me wonder. . . . Did everyone there know him? Had he made friends with people?

She wrote on: "A wicker basket containing some linen belonging to Mr. Rosen has been left in the room, which had been sealed up by the Gendarmes." In this room, Madame Bobières wrote, "is my furniture, including a large cupboard, containing [. . .] sheets, clothes, linen, blankets, and family papers."

So she was asking for belongings back from Martin's room—which was still sealed.

As for Martin's belongings, Madame Bobières added, "Rosen's brother-in-law who lives in the next room, and who is French, could look after the wicker basket, which is the only piece of furniture belonging to Rosen."

Here was something that set my mind racing. If Martin had a brother-in-law who was French, that surely meant Martin had a French wife!

Who was she? What was her name? Was there anybody alive who knew anything about her?

Since the British edition of this book was published, I discovered that Oscar-Jeschie and Martin were soldiers on opposite sides of the First World War. They might have fought each other. But there's more: according to another document, Martin was the best man at Oscar-Jeschie's wedding to Rachel, just a few years later. But there's still a lot left to find out . . .

I was really surprised when the report said that Martin was a jeweler. The family story had always been that he was a dentist! I'd like to know more, but haven't found anything else yet.

You might also be wondering why Martin's surname appears as both "Rozen" and "Rosen." I think it's just because when people went from country to country, like Martin, they sometimes changed the way they spelled their names.

There's also that matter of this brother-in-law—and, I assume, of his wife. Will I ever find out about them?

I don't know. But at least I have found out all this.

Oscar and Martin's names are engraved on the Shoah Memorial, in Paris.

Which means that they won't be forgotten. The Nazis may have succeeded in killing them, but they can't kill their memory.

And now I've told you about them. So, as the French would say, *Souviens-toi.*

Remember.

Martin Rozen (1890–1944)

My Father's Uncle

On January 31, 1944,

at 2:30 in the morning

in a village in France,

four policemen knock on the door

of a woman

who has several lodgers in her house.

They take away one of them,

a man

who has done nothing wrong.

They take him to a nearby town

to put him with thirty others

who have done nothing wrong.

He is taken away with them
and put on a train
to where he and they are put
with hundreds of others
who have done nothing wrong.

He is then taken away by a train
carrying more than a thousand people
to another country
where he is put with thousands
and thousands of others
who have done nothing wrong.
And killed.

14

One of my great-uncles was a clock mender and another was a jeweler. That's all they did wrong—which is to say, they did nothing wrong. And yet, they died for being who they were.

When we talk about the Holocaust, people often say, "Never again." That what happened to my great-uncles, and the millions of other people systematically killed by the Nazis, must never, ever happen again. But we have to ask ourselves: How many attempts at genocide have there been since? The answer is quite a few.

Many more people have been through what Michael, Olga, and Ted went through: losing people they loved. And of course, many more people have been through what my great-aunts and great-uncles went through: knowing that you are being killed for no other reason than being who you are.

Some people think the Holocaust was intended right from the start. Others think that it came about as a result of Nazi Germany invading other countries—Poland in particular. That this turned the Nazis from persecution and murder to genocide.

When you really look at the history of it all, you can see that these terrible things happened bit by bit: in stages.

What was going on in Germany in, say, the 1920s was not the same as what was happening in 1944, when the mass killings were taking place. So now people look for signs of what might be a dangerous slippery slope.

We have words like *racism, prejudice, antisemitism, xenophobia, discrimination,* and *supremacism* to describe these first steps; they all mean slightly different things.

I'm very concerned about the prejudice I see today—all the more so because of what happened to my family. It's not that I think it's going to happen again tomorrow; it's that, if I'd been alive in 1940, it would have happened to me.

With every passing year, the number of Holocaust survivors gets smaller. We need to keep the memory of them alive: the people who died and those who survived. That's partly why I wrote this book.

But it's not the only reason. Because I'm concerned not just about antisemitism but about all the ways in which groups of people become targets of hatred.

Especially when there's a government involved, feeding those feelings or even starting to "legally" discriminate against people. Dividing people up by religion or race. Splitting up families.

And turning away people with nowhere else to go—like the millions of refugees forced to leave their homes in Syria in recent years. Forced to travel on foot, in trucks, on boats, for thousands of miles. Men, women, and children.

People like me or you.

Clock menders and jewelers.

I want to end this book with a poem of mine that I'm very fond of.

I wrote it after looking at photos of Jews who had been imprisoned in a ghetto in Poland. One of them showed a couple smiling and staring up at a tree.

It felt unbearable to know (while they didn't) that they were going to die. But these people were full of joy . . .

I wanted to express this in a poem. I thought of despair and hope—hope and despair.

Which way round should they go? I wondered.

I knew the answer. We can't live on despair: we always have to find reason to hope. Because the world doesn't have to be this way.

More than that, we can't let it.

So turn the page for "Today; One Day."

Today; One Day

Today

The rain has died

My shoes have died

The sun has died

My coat has died

The Earth has died

Today.

One day

The rain will flower

My shoes will laugh

The sun will sing

My coat will fly

The Earth will dance

One day.

FURTHER READING

Firsthand accounts of World War II and the Holocaust

- Frank, Anne. *The Diary of a Young Girl: The Definitive Edition*. Edited by Otto H. Frank and Mirjam Pressler. Translated by Susan Massotty. Illustrated by Harry Brockway. Puffin Books, 1997. Age 8 and up.

- Greenfeld, Howard. *The Hidden Children*. Houghton Mifflin Harcourt, 1993. Age 10 and up.

- Gut Opdyke, Irene. *In My Hands: Memories of a Holocaust Rescuer*. With Jennifer Armstrong. Corgi Children's, 2009. Age 8 and up.

- Joffo, Joseph. *A Bag of Marbles*. Translated by Martin Sokolinsky. University of Chicago Press, 2001. Age 8 and up.

- Matthews, Stephen. *The Day the Nazis Came: The Astonishing True Story of a Childhood Journey from the Occupied Channel Islands to the Dark Heart of a German Prison Camp*. John Blake Publishing, 2016.

- Toll, Nelly S. *Behind the Secret Window: A Memoir of a Hidden Childhood During World War Two.* Puffin Books, 1993. Age 8 and up.

Children's nonfiction about World War II and the Holocaust

- Bauer, Yehuda. *A History of the Holocaust.* Revised edition. Children's Press, 1982, updated 2001. Age 12 and up.

- Freedman, Russell. *We Will Not Be Silent: The White Rose Student Resistance Movement That Defied Adolf Hitler.* Clarion Books, 2016. Age 8 and up.

- Herman, Gail, and Who HQ. *What Was the Holocaust?* What Was? series. Illustrated by Jerry Hoare. Penguin Random House, 2018. Age 8 and up.

- Levine, Karen. *Hana's Suitcase: The Quest to Solve a Holocaust Mystery.* Crown Books for Young Readers, 2016. Age 8 and up.

- Rappaport, Doreen. *Beyond Courage: The Untold Story of Jewish Resistance During the Holocaust*. Candlewick Press, 2014. Age 12 and up.

- Thomson, Ruth. *Terezín: Voices from the Holocaust*. Candlewick Press, 2013. Age 10 and up.

- *Voices from the Second World War: Stories of War as Told to Children of Today*. Candlewick Press, 2018. Ages 10–14.

For further information on World War II and the Holocaust online

- The Anne Frank Center for Mutual Respect
  WWW.ANNEFRANK.COM

- The Holocaust Educational Trust
  WWW.HET.ORG.UK

- Mémorial de la Shoah (The Shoah Memorial)
  WWW.MEMORIALDELASHOAH.ORG/EN

- The United States Holocaust Memorial Museum
  WWW.USHMM.ORG

- The Wiener Holocaust Library
  WWW.WIENERLIBRARY.CO.UK

- Yad Vashem: The World Holocaust
  Remembrance Center
  WWW.YADVASHEM.ORG

Children's fiction about World War II and the Holocaust

- Adlington, Lucy. *The Red Ribbon*. Candlewick Press, 2018. Age 12 and up.

- Gleitzman, Morris. *Once*. Puffin Books, 2006. Age 9 and up.

- Janeczko, Paul B. *Requiem: Poems of the Terezín Ghetto*. Candlewick Press, 2011. Age 12 and up.

- Kerr, Judith. *When Hitler Stole Pink Rabbit*. Illustrated by the author. HarperCollins, 1971. Age 9 and up.

- Macdonald, Maryann. *Odette's Secrets*. Bloomsbury, 2013. Age 9 and up.

- Naidoo, Beverley. *The Other Side of Truth*. Puffin Books, 2007. Age 9 and up.

- Toksvig, Sandi. *Hitler's Canary*. Yearling, 2006. Age 9 and up.

- Yolen, Jane. *The Devil's Arithmetic*. Puffin Books, 2004. Age 10 and up.

- Zail, Suzy. *Playing for the Commandant*. Candlewick Press, 2014. Age 12 and up.

Children's nonfiction about refugees and displacement

- Matthews, Jenny. *Children Growing Up with War*. Candlewick Press, 2014. Ages 10–14.

- McCarney, Rosemary. *Where Will I Live?* With images by the United Nations High Commissioner for Refugees. Second Story Press, 2017. Age 4 and up.

- Roberts, Ceri. *Children in Our World: Refugees and Migrants*. Illustrated by Hanane Kai. Wayland, 2016. Age 6 and up.

- Rosen, Michael, and Annemarie Young. *Who Are Refugees and Migrants? What Makes People Leave Their Homes? And Other Big Questions*. Wayland, 2016. Age 7 and up.

Children's fiction about refugees and displacement

- Fraillon, Zana. *The Bone Sparrow*. Orion Children's Books, 2016. Age 12 and up.

- Fraillon, Zana. *The Ones That Disappeared*. Orion Children's Books, 2017. Age 12 and up.

- Geda, Fabio. *In the Sea There Are Crocodiles: The Story of Enaiatollah Akbari*. Translated by Howard Curtis. David Fickling Books, 2011. Age 10 and up.

- Laird, Elizabeth. *Welcome to Nowhere*. Macmillan Children's Books, 2017. Age 9 and up.

- Lewis, Gill. *A Story Like the Wind*. Illustrated by Jo Weaver. Oxford University Press, 2017. Age 8 and up.

- Zephaniah, Benjamin. *Refugee Boy*. Bloomsbury, 2001. Age 12 and up.

Picture books about World War II and the Holocaust

- Gottesfeld, Jeff. *The Tree in the Courtyard: Looking Through Anne Frank's Window*. Illustrated by Peter McCarty. Knopf Books for Young Readers, 2016. Age 5 and up.

- Russo, Marisabina. *I Will Come Back for You: A Family in Hiding During World War II*. Illustrated by the author. Schwartz & Wade, 2011. Age 6 and up.

- Wiviott, Meg. *Benno and the Night of Broken Glass*. Illustrated by Josée Bisaillon. Kar-Ben Publishing, 2010. Age 5 and up.

Picture books about refugees and displacement

- Booth, Anne. *Refuge*. Illustrated by Sam Usher. Nosy Crow, 2015. Age 3 and up.

- Davies, Nicola. *The Day War Came*. Illustrated by Rebecca Cobb. Candlewick Press, 2018. Age 5 and up.

- Hoffman, Mary. *The Color of Home*. Illustrated by Karin Littlewood. Phyllis Fogelman Books, 2002. Age 3 and up.

- Milner, Kate. *My Name Is Not Refugee*. Illustrated by the author. The Bucket List, 2017. Age 5 and up.

- Sanna, Francesca. *The Journey*. Illustrated by the author. Flying Eye Books, 2016. Age 5 and up.

- Wild, Margaret. *The Treasure Box*. Illustrated by Freya Blackwood. Candlewick Press, 2017. Ages 5–8.

Graphic novels about World War II and the Holocaust

- Dauvillier, Loïc. *Hidden: A Child's Story of the Holocaust*. Illustrated by Marc Lizano and Greg Salsedo. First Second, 2014. Age 6 and up.

- Shackleton, Kath, ed. *Survivors of the Holocaust*. Illustrated by Zane Whittingham. Sourcebooks Explore, 2019. Age 9 and up.

- Spiegelman, Art. *Maus: A Survivor's Tale. Vol. I, My Father Bleeds History*. Illustrated by the author. Pantheon Books, 1991.

- Spiegelman, Art. *Maus: A Survivor's Tale. Vol. II, And Here My Troubles Began*. Illustrated by the author. Pantheon Books, 1991.

Graphic novels about refugees and displacement

- Bessora. *Alpha: Abidjan to Gare du Nord.*
  Illustrated by Barroux. Translated by Sarah
  Ardizzone. The Bucket List, 2016. Age 11
  and up.

- Colfer, Eoin, and Andrew Donkin. *Illegal:
  One Boy's Epic Journey of Hope and Survival.*
  Illustrated by Giovanni Rigano. Hodder
  Children's Books, 2017. Age 8 and up.

- Tan, Shaun. *The Arrival.* Illustrated by the
  author. Hodder Children's Books, 2007.
  Age 5 and up.

Audio

I have also recorded poems about my family's experience of the Holocaust and poems about racism and prejudice; these recordings are freely available via Historyworks on Audioboom:

HTTPS://AUDIOBOOM.COM/PLAYLISTS /4613930-MICHAEL-ROSEN-POEMS

INDEX

ACKNOWLEDGMENTS

The lines of poetry titled "Not Just for Them" on pages iv, 31, and 80 were first published in *Don't Mention the Children* by Michael Rosen (Smokestack Books, 2015); the lines titled "Dear Oscar" on pages 70–72 were first published in *Listening to a Pogrom on the Radio* by Michael Rosen (Smokestack Books, 2017). "Skeletons" was reproduced from *Quick, Let's Get Out of Here* by Michael Rosen (Puffin Books). Copyright © by Michael Rosen 1983. "Bagel," "On the Move Again," and "Today; One Day" were reproduced from *Michael Rosen's Big Book of Bad Things* by Michael Rosen (Puffin Books). Copyright © by Michael Rosen 2010. "Names" was reproduced from *Jelly Boots, Smelly Boots* by Michael Rosen (Bloomsbury, 2016) and is printed by permission of Bloomsbury Publishing Plc on behalf of Michael Rosen. Every effort has been made to secure permission for the use of copyrighted material. If notified of any omission, the editor and publisher will gladly make the necessary correction in future printings.

Thanks also to **L'Harmattan**, publishers of *Destin à Part: Seul déporté rescapé de la rafle de Clans du*

25 octobre 1943 by Henry Bily; **Les Archives de la Vendée**; **Robert Laffont**, publishers of *J'ai pas pleuré* by Ida Grinspan and Bertrand Poirot-Delpech; **Geste éditions**, publishers of *Les Chemins de la honte: Itinéraire d'une persécution, Deux-Sèvres 1940–1944* by Jean-Marie Pouplain; **Klarsfeld**, publishers of *Le Mémorial de la déportation des Juifs de France* by Serge Klarsfeld; **Éditions les Chantuseries**, publishers of *La traque: Le destin des Juifs de Vendée pendant la seconde guerre mondiale* by Louis Gouraud; **Éditions du centre**, publishers of *Jews Under the Italian Occupation* by Léon Poliakov and Jacques Sabille; and the online publication of "Récit de Philippe Glanzberg."

And special thanks to: **Nadia Hassani** for translating the letters from Oscar and Stella; **Teddy Rosen** for sharing the discoveries of the letters and photos; **Professor Helen Weinstein** and **Historyworks**, Cambridge, England, for their work for Holocaust Memorial Day, my work with them in schools, and Helen's comments on this book; **Associate Professor Andy Pearce** from the UCL

Centre for Holocaust Education, for reading the manuscript and being so generous with his time; **Nicola Wetherall MBE** from the UCL Centre for Holocaust Education for her help; **the Wiener Library** for their archive of Holocaust documents, and for the photo on page 32; **the American Jewish Historical Society**, New England Archives; **Mémorial de la Shoah**, Paris; **Gérald Dardart**, historian of the Ardennes during the Second World War; my French teachers, especially **Keith** and the late **Thelma Emmans** at Watford Boys Grammar School; **Caroline Royds**, who championed this book from the beginning; the late **Ted Rosen** and **Olga Rosen**; **Michael** and **Grant Rechnic**; and the late **Harold** and **Connie Rosen**, my parents, for telling me what they knew and didn't know.